IN THE CRADLE OF GOD'S ARMS

SANDRA A. FERGINS

In the Cradle Of God's Arms
Copyright @ 2021 by Sandra A. Fergins

All rights reserved.
Without limiting the rights under copyright law, no part of this publication may be produced, stored or introduced into a retrieval system, or transmitted, in any form or by any (electronic, mechanical, photocopying, recording or otherwise), without the prior written permission of both the copyright owner and publisher, except brief quotations embodied in critical reviews and certain other noncommercial uses permitted by copyright law.

All scripture from the King James Version of the Holy Bible.

ISBN: 978-1-7360013-9-4

ACKNOWLEDGMENTS

I thank the Lord for his love and daily guidance.
Thank you to my husband Michael for his listening ear
and making me laugh! I also thank my publisher,
Cedric D. Fisher and his team for their tireless efforts
in the production of my second book!

Ephesians 6:24
Grace be with all them that love our Lord Jesus Christ in sincerity. Amen

John 14:27
Peace I leave with you, my peace I give unto you:not as the world giveth, give I unto you. Let not your heart be troubled, neither let it be afraid.

TABLE OF CONTENTS

Acknowledgments	3	Life's Cycle	36
About the Author	9	His GPS	37
The Angels	11	Keep Standing	38
He's There	12	Keep Him In Your Day	39
You Are Blessed	13	Hangups	40
Trust Him	14	Longing for Christ	41
He's Coming	15	He Sees Us All	42
Live Life	16	Let Me Grow	43
Serve Him	17	No More	44
Sunday Morning	18	Warning!!	45
It's Gonna Be All Right	19	My Hero!!	46
Find freedom with Jesus	20	His Plan	47
Would You?	21	My Strong Tower	48
He Is Right There	22	Many Thanks	49
Keep praying	23	Look	50
Another life loss	24	No Failure In God	51
The Storm	25	Lights, Camera, Action!!	52
He's here for you	26	Those Negative Days	53
Behold Glory Surrounds	27	Keep the faith	54
Why? Why?	28	This Life Will End	55
Things	30	The Year 2020	56
I Need Your Strength	31	Give the Highest Praise	57
Sickness	32	A Story	58
Look To Him	33	He will carry your problems	59
Worship	34	Fear	60
One More Day	35	Thank You	61

In The Cradle Of God's Arms

Be Careful	62	In His Arms	94
He's Coming Back	63	Your Answer Is Coming	95
What A Happy Day!	64	Stay Ready	96
Reach Out	65	Blessed	97
Serve, Live, Try Him	66	Shelter From The Storms	98
No One Like You	67	It's Okay	100
Stay Strong	68	Look To Him	101
Be Grateful	69	Blessed Beyond Measure	102
A journey	70	The Rain	103
Power	71	Guide Me	104
A Blessing	72	No Win	105
Death	73	The Right Path	106
Why?	74	Unity	107
Just Wait	75	A Problem Solver	108
God's Creation	76	There For Us	109
Time	77	The Rain	110
Get Back	78	In The Cradle Of God's Arms	111
What's Happening	79		
God's Peace	80	Hope	112
A Friend's Life Has Ended	81	Better Days	113
A Bright And Wonderful Day	82	Christ Can Fix It	114
		None Other	115
Our Heavenly Home	83	The Bible	116
Look Up	84	In His Arms	117
Another Day	85	Connect	118
Your Answer	86	God's There	119
Wait	87	Gone Away	120
There For You	88	Waiting For You	121
A Day	89	He's Here For Us	122
The Best Is Yet To Come	90	It's Coming	123
Children	91	Gone On	124
He's Calling Us	92	Feelings	125
Wake Up	93	Mother	126

Sandra A. Fergins

Daughters	127
Snow	128
Plop!	129
Awake	130
A Better Day	131
Troubles Don't Last	132
Grateful	133
There For You	134
Gone Away	135
My Children	136
Faith	137
Seeking Answers	138
Lonely Trials	139
Look Forward	140
Surrender	141
You Matter To God	142
Life?? Death??	143
Pain	144
Grief	145
Childhood	146
AllieRay (My Youngest Grandson Allieray Searcy)	147
The Bible	148
There For You	149
In His Time	150
Water	151
Nature	152
The Hospital	153
His Love	154
If.	155
Looking For Peace	156
That Hopeless Feeling	157
There For You	158
Tell It	159
An Ending	160
What Are You Waiting For	161
Marriage	162
Trees	163
Nature	164
Rain	165
Lightning	166
Old Age	167
The Reunion	169
There For You	171
Help	172
Shoes	173
A Miracle	174
Stop The Violence	175
A Teacher	176
Wrong Person	178
The Covid Blues	179
Get Right	181
Skit	182
The Unexpected Event	182
Skit 2	186
The Change	186

*In the cradle of
God's arms*

*Security can
be found*

*His tenderness
gently surrounds*

*Keeping us from
hurt or harm*

Sandra A. Fergins

ABOUT THE AUTHOR

Sandra Fergins holds a Master's and Bachelor's degree from Texas State University. She is a retired music teacher from Fort Sam Houston Elementary School. She was a part of that district for twenty-one wonderful years. Sandra simply loved to see her students perform and showcased many musicals along with the help of colleagues and parents that included singing, acting, costumes, dancing and beautiful backdrops for all to enjoy. It was a thrill to her to see the final production come to fruition.

Before working at Fort Sam Houston Elementary school Sandra worked at Menchaca Elementary in Austin, Texas for nineteen years as a music teacher. Her first music teaching position was at Carl Schurz Elementary in New Braunfels, Texas.

Sandra loves to sing, play the piano, write poems and music. She has completed two gospel albums that have received airplay on the radio, "Pray and There's No Better

Friend...Jesus. She also has one of the songs "There's No Better Friend...Jesus" on YouTube.

Sandra's husband is a real estate broker and teacher of real estate classes for the Alamo College District. Michael and Sandra started their own real estate company "Fergins & Associates Realty" in 1999. They were influenced to go into the real estate business by Sandra's dad Howard L. Shelf who has been an icon in real estate for over sixty years. Her mom, Angeline Shelf, retired from interior design work.

Sandra has two sisters and one brother. Angela Medearis has written popular children's books and many cookbooks. She even won a cook off against Bobby Flay! Marcia Orlandi is a real estate broker and also loves to cook and cater. Her brother, Howard Shelf II is also a real estate broker and music teacher. Sandra has four children: Kendra Searcy, Kenneth Prosser, Michael Fergins, Jr. and Marcy Fergins. She has eight grandchildren Dezarae Fernandez, Julissa Castillo, Charles Fergins, Kenneth Jackson, Reginal Ryan, Jaylen Allen, Rocco DeMore and AllieRay Searcy.

Sandra A. Fergins

THE ANGELS

Many things we do not know
The angels are keeping us safe
We walk in fear not knowing what's ahead
The angels are keeping us safe
The Lord is above
The creator of all
He commissions the angels to keep us safe

My husband Michael and I

HE'S THERE

In the morning in the evening at noonday
He's there
My God is waiting patiently just call
He cares
He's a healer, a fixer of the greatest problem you can have
Don't be afraid to ask for help
His love abounds all around

Sandra A. Fergins

YOU ARE BLESSED

You don't know how blessed you are to be able to walk, talk, move
and **complain**
You don't know how grateful you should be to see one more day the good Lord has brought your way
You don't know how happy you should be to receive His mercy, love and kindness each and every day
You don't know how thankful you should be to really comprehend the life and protection my God has extended to the creature He created in the form of
man, woman and child
Show Him you know by showing love
Show Him you know by showing kindness
Show Him you know by walking and talking daily with Him
Show Him when you do show these traits
The world will see not you but…….Him

TRUST HIM

The Lord is beyond good
He is incomprehensible
In Him we find true love
We find unconditional love
There is no one like Him and never will be
He is someone you can put all your trust and belief in
Man will let you down because man doesn't have the same strength as God
That is why **HE** is called God
Show the world He lives each and every day you have breath

Sandra A. Fergins

HE'S COMING

One day I will bow at my Savior's feet
To honor and glorify Him we will meet
To praise His holy name
Life will never be the same
For to live with a being so powerful, magnificent, holy and supreme is
indescribable to a creature created by Him
We have so much to look forward to for
that evil world has now been left far behind
The saints of God will be loving, marvelous and oh so kind
What a day! What a day! What a day!

In The Cradle Of God's Arms

LIVE LIFE

Life is here
live it to its fullest
You begin and end it quickly sometimes
The Lord giveth and He taketh away
We have no say in the matter

My daughter-in-law, son and grandson Bobbi Prosser, Kenneth Prosser and AllieRay Searcey

Sandra A. Fergins

SERVE HIM

When sickness comes we feel so bad
When our health is restored we feel quite glad
Serve the Lord whether you are up or down
Give Him His glory whether glad or sad
He gave you one more day of praise

In The Cradle Of God's Arms

SUNDAY MORNING

Sunday morning
What a day
People gather from every which way
Strolling in smiling and waving
Others come in, you know they need saving
An array of outfits the sisters are wearing
The latest news they laugh and love sharing
Some brothers gather chatting in the hall
They reach out quickly to aid an elder who was about to trip and fall
The children tag one another and giggle
They quickly receive a stern look from mom and know not to wiggle
The pastor soon brings the message for the week
It is comforting with the strength we seek
Soon back to our homes we go
To practice and study God's word we love so

Sandra A. Fergins

IT'S GONNA BE ALL RIGHT

The Lord has your back
He keeps life intact
Whenever it looks like we may go astray
He leads us to a positive way
Whenever life makes you feel you are about to drown
The Lord will not let you stay down, down, down
Look up things will get better

When life seems that it's not going your way
Look to Jesus for that love you miss

Love is a powerful word and action
Pass it on today

FIND FREEDOM WITH JESUS

Shackled by a world of sin
Pain so deep your soul within
Problems with others you hate to share
Deep inside you feel they don't care
Rage so strong you feel you are about to burst
You feel your life is oh so cursed
Turn it all over to the Master above
He's waiting for you….with arms of love

Sandra A. Fergins

WOULD YOU?

He died on calvary's tree
He gave His love for you and me
All of this for mankind so that we could be free
Would you give your life for me?
Would you hang upon that tree?
His love has been proven beyond heights and depths
Reach out to the Lord
Reach out, reach out
He is waiting to heal your pain
Accept Him
Peace you will gain
Walk in His path today

HE IS RIGHT THERE

The Lord is beyond good
He is incomprehensible
In Him we find true love we find unconditional love
There is no one like Him and never will be
He is someone you can put all your trust and belief in
Man will let you down because man doesn't have the same strength as
God
That is why He is called God
Show the world He lives each and every day you have breath

Sandra A. Fergins

KEEP PRAYING

Depression, rejection, hate and scorn
Spewing out of the hearts of man towards others
We look around and wonder why
The world is in such a despicable mess
Countries despising one another
Killings, divisions, hate crimes daily
Some in a doped up unnatural sex mess
We need to pray, pray and pray some more
For the Lord to forgive our ungrateful ways

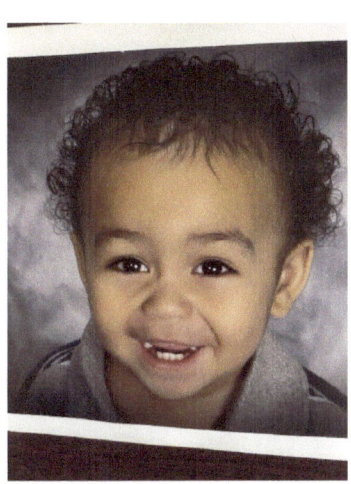

Charles Fergins, my grandson

ANOTHER LIFE LOSS

Another life has come and gone
at the hand of a common citizen or police officer
that same old song
So sad to hear of your loss
for all to witness such a dreadful cost
Through tears and heaviness we go through our day
Searching for answers and the right thing to say
Hold your head up high look to the sky
One day to our wonderful maker
We will fly, fly fly

Sandra A. Fergins

THE STORM

On a dark and stormy night
You hear God's voice in the rolling thunder
and the flashing, flickering lights
You recoil in fear as the storm draws near
but in His sweet soft voice He gently says
I am here, I am here
Nature I command from the raging seas to the gentle sands
Lean on me and do not fear
I am here, I am here

Proverbs 22:2
The rich and poor meet together: the Lord is the maker of them all.

Proverbs 15:16
Better is little with the fear of the Lord than great treasure and trouble therewith.

In The Cradle Of God's Arms

HE'S HERE FOR YOU

Believe He'll do it
Receive His blessings
The Lord is here
To help you through your good days and bad
To guide you through this maze called life
To hold you up
He hears your humble call

Sandra A. Fergins

BEHOLD GLORY SURROUNDS

Nature what a sight to behold
Bees flitting here and there gathering nectar
Flowers blooming in all their glory so colorful
Fruit trees changing colors in a wondrous display
ready to release their bounty of food
The Lord in all His glory you can witness in nature
Friends what a glorious sight we have yet to behold

My dad, Howard L. Shelf I, on his 92 birthday

In The Cradle Of God's Arms

WHY? WHY?

Why is there so much hatred in this world?
God has allowed this for a season
Why can't races get along?
We are all from the same bloodline
Love will reign one day.
Why do the storms wreck havoc and destruction?
It is only because God allows it.
He is in control of the seas and the winds.
Why do we have to die?
The Lord has only predestined our lives for a season.
While we have this life, how will you use it?
Will you abuse it through drugs, drinks and smokes?
Will you lift His name for all to hear?
Will you call on Him when life brings fear?
Will you trust Him when you don't understand?
Why, why, why not let go of whatever holds you back
and let God lead you today.
Why, not?

Sandra A. Fergins

Philippians 4:9
Those things, which ye have both learned, and received, and heard, and seen in me, do: and the God of peace shall be with you.

THINGS

Things here, things there
Things, things everywhere
Do we really need those things we see
Or should we walk away and let them be
A material item that will soon pass away
Something we work for day to day
Let it go
Let it be
The thrill will pass
Soon you will see

Sandra A. Fergins

I NEED YOUR STRENGTH

I want to see you Lord in peace
Please accept my humble plea
People put up roadblocks every now and then
Help me to look for your strength daily to get
through and stay free
Sometimes I get in my own way
Help me to lean on your word to guide me
day to day come what may

SICKNESS

My, my, sickness
It has its purpose
To bring you closer to God and those around
He knows how to get your attention
Sometimes through light affliction or a heavy one
My God will keep you praying to please lift this sickness
Please, please lift it
He knows what He's doing and in due time sometimes it goes gently away
Other times it may linger on
Sickness…...

My, my sickness

Showered with blessings from God above
So undeserving of His love.

Look around, look around a good life
can be found.

Sandra A. Fergins

LOOK TO HIM

One day I will bow at my savior's feet
To honor and glorify Him we will meet
To praise His holy name
Life will never be the same
For to live with a being so powerful, magnificent, holy and supreme is indescribable to a creature created by Him
We have so much to look forward to that evil world left far behind
The saints of God will be loving, marvelous and oh so kind
What a day!
What a day!
What a day!

WORSHIP

Come to worship God in all His greatness
He deserves more than we can imagine
Stand, shout, dance, scream
He's worth it
We can't do enough

Sandra A. Fergins

ONE MORE DAY

One more day you gave to me
One more day I'm able to see
One more day to worship and praise
One more day to walk through this world's maze
Thank you, thank you Lord for giving me one more day.

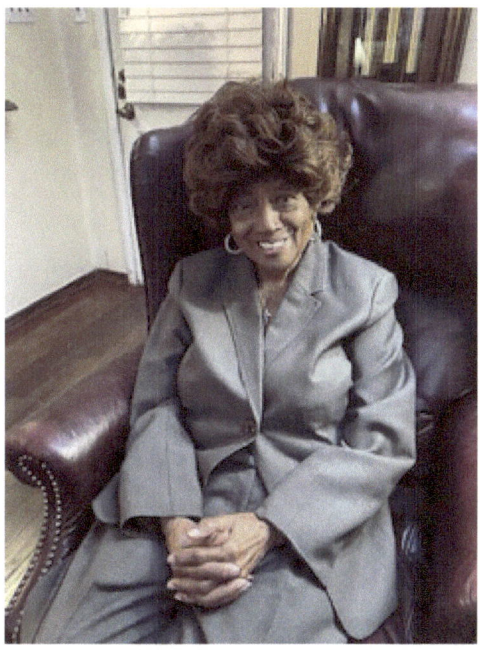

My beautiful mom, Angeline Shelf.

In The Cradle Of God's Arms

LIFE'S CYCLE

Life and death go hand in hand
Events sometimes we don't understand
God created a destination for all
One day we all will heed His call
Life begins when He commands
Death takes place when He demands
Are you ready for the cycle we all will go through?

Sandra A. Fergins

HIS GPS

While riding by car a **GPS** can take us many places near and far

God's **P**lan of **S**alvation shows us how to reach Him in the most treacherous times

We may be going through a downturn

His plan may say look up and get right you don't want to burn

We may be going through sickness

His plan may say lean on me be patient don't live in fright

We may be overwhelmed with grief

His plan may say wait, stand still, soon I'll be sending relief

KEEP STANDING

He was despised and rejected of men
Yet He still stood
He was bruised, mocked and scoffed for what He came for
Yet He still stood
He was heckled, beat and many had unbelief
Yet He still stood
Stand for your belief in Christ come what may from day to day
Your day to prove your love is coming soon

Sandra A. Fergins

KEEP HIM IN YOUR DAY

It's cold outside
It's hot outside
It's often in between
The weather has a great effect on our daily activities
Don't leave the Lord out of your day today

HANGUPS

Sometimes life sends us hangups
We feel grouchy, moody out of whack
Pray to get your calm self back

Sandra A. Fergins

LONGING FOR CHRIST

Keep me in your care
Your loving words help me to share
There is none like you
nor ever will be
Your marvelous kingdom I long to see

Vanessa Kennedy, former co-worker

HE SEES US ALL

God is looking down
Some things He sees brings on a frown
Sin, sin and more sin
Don't get deeper and keep doing it again
Read His word to keep your conscious clean
When you stray away it makes you weaker, vulnerable and mean
Lift the Savior up while you have life
Show the world you don't have to live in bitter envy, grief and strife

Sandra A. Fergins

LET ME GROW

The warm place I rest in your body is the place I want to be
Please don't disturb me
Don't take this place away from me
I was placed there to grow inside you month by month week by week, day by day
Life is given by the Lord above no matter what man may say
Let me be in time you will see a beautiful life was formed to behold
In time I will return your love
As gently in your arms you hold me

NO MORE

Cut off from this life on earth through sickness, age or someone's rage

Cutoff to spend time with loved one's here on earth, oh no,

Please say it isn't so

Are they all really cut off

No the Lord just sends His warning to the living

That you only have so many days on earth that He's willing to be giving

Sandra A. Fergins

WARNING!!

Newsflash!
Listen up! Diseases
Wake up! Floods
Tune in! Pestilences
Observe! Death
The world is in turmoil
Uproar! Sin, sin everywhere
My Lord speaks through these devastations
happening all around
He doesn't want to lose not one of His creation
He sends these warnings out to please heed, please heed
Get ready, He says, I'm coming back
Please don't procrastinate
Get your life in order
I'm coming sooner than you think!!!

MY HERO!!

God is my hero
He can move mountains and make a way out of no way
God is my hero
He can heal when the doctor's are at wits end and give you life again
God is my hero
He can bring joy, laughter and uplift a lost soul
Bring families together that once fell into a divided drift
God is my hero
There is none like Him and never will be
Don't look to man to solve your problems and grief
Look to God, Jesus Christ and His angels to send your needed relief

GOD IS MY HERO!!

Sandra A. Fergins

HIS PLAN

Life is what you make it
No, God has already delivered His plan
Your life is like a road map
You have to follow
Let God be part of your plan and your life will be so much happier

Habakkuk 3:18
Yet I will rejoice in the Lord, I will joy in the God of my salvation.

Psalms 33:21
For our heart shall rejoice in him, because we have trusted in his holy name.

MY STRONG TOWER

Man you have no power
Jesus Christ is my strong tower
Life is but for a season
Living for Christ is a wonderful reason
Do your best
He'll supply the rest
We're here on earth but for a short while
Show Jesus you want to be His loving child

Sandra A. Fergins

MANY THANKS

Lord I thank you for my happy days and sad ones too
You've given me life and a work here on earth to do
With your strength I can accomplish those goals
By reaching out near and far to many lost souls

Howard Shelf, Angeline Shelf, Sandra Fergins, Stephanie Tyree, Marcia Orlandi, Evan Orlandi and Aydan Hagler

LOOK

Look at His side
Look at His feet
Look at the nails driven into His hands
Christ endured all of this because of the great love He had for us
Can we endure problems, sickness and the unknown ahead
to show our love for Him too

Please the Lord it will bring God a wonderful smile.

II Peter 3:18
But grow in grace, and in the knowledge of our Lord and Savior Jesus Christ. To him be glory both now and for ever. Amen

Proverbs 3:5, 6
Trust in the Lord with all thine heart; and lean not unto thine own understanding.
In all thy ways acknowledge him, and he shall direct thy paths.

Sandra A. Fergins

NO FAILURE IN GOD

Joy comes from within
Please the Lord get rid of sin
Feeling down, leveled to the ground
Look to Jesus
Happiness can be found
Are you perplexed
Don't know what's happening next
My God is in control over all creation
and of every nation
Don't despair, He is fully aware
of sickness, plagues, life and death
He will not fail
Keep praying
He will not fail

In The Cradle Of God's Arms

LIGHTS, CAMERA, ACTION!!

Lights
The world is in turmoil
People in a panic
Gripped with fear far and near

Camera
God is here
He sees your need through His ever watching eye
Focusing on the picture below

Action
He sends His love from above telling us
always keep still
Keep still I am here for you

Sandra A. Fergins

THOSE NEGATIVE DAYS

A negative spirit drags you down
Leaves you with an endless frown
Bad thoughts, bad vibes spew endlessly throughout the day
Pray fast so that feeling will not last
A brighter day awaits
When......

That negative feeling out you cast

KEEP THE FAITH

Keep your faith in the storm
Keep your faith in a plague
No matter what is thrown your way stand up for what you believe
The devil will attack you no matter which way you turn
Remember God is able to help you withstand and will lend His guiding hand
He is there for us and will never let us down
Trust Him
Believe His word
Stay strong through the storm
Don't believe every lie the media throws your way
Their lies are meant to weaken your faith
Come what may
Dear Christian read His word pray fervently
Lean on Christ and lean some more
He said I will never leave you nor forsake you
Cling to those loving words
Keep your faith in the storm
Keep your faith in a plague

Sandra A. Fergins

THIS LIFE WILL END

One more month
One more week
One more day has come our way
How quickly the hours, the minutes, the seconds fly away
Treasure this life the Lord has given us all
For one day it will come to a
SCREECHING HALT!!

In The Cradle Of God's Arms

THE YEAR 2020

2020 what a year
filled with sickness, death and fear
Newscasts blaring day in and out
Destruction, disease, fire, tornadoes, calamities, fightings, death all about
We must hold fast to what we believe
For living eternally with Jesus is the greatest accomplishment we can ever achieve

Sandra A. Fergins

GIVE THE HIGHEST PRAISE

Praise Him in the highest
Bend down on your knees
Look up with grateful praise
He alone is our deliverer

My brother, Howard L. Shelf 11, sister-in-law, Evonne Shelf and their granddaughter Harmony McGarity

A STORY

Your story
My story
But....the greatest story ever told was that of Jesus Christ
Though He only lived but a short while
His story impacted the whole wide world

Amen, amen, amen

Sandra A. Fergins

HE WILL CARRY YOUR PROBLEMS

Cast your fears upon the Lord
He will help you carry them

Cast aside your fearful heart
The Lord heareth your cry

Cast aside your doubting, fearful ways
The Lord is able to uplift you in your
time of need

In The Cradle Of God's Arms

FEAR

Fear is felt all around
Fear can level you to the ground
Fear the Lord
He will help you when you are at wits end
His forever comfort
He will send

*My daughter, Kendra Searcey and her children.
Reginal Ryan and Dezarae Fernandez*

Sandra A. Fergins

THANK YOU

Thank you Lord for health and strength
Something I often take too lightly
It is you that gave it to me not me Lord, not me
I can do nothing without you
Nothing, nothing, nothing at all
You guide me through my ups
You love me through my downs
You are my comforter
No one can love and care for me like you Lord
No one…..
No one at all

In The Cradle Of God's Arms

BE CAREFUL

Trouble is all around
The devil never sleeps
Watch constantly
Watch, pray without ceasing
The Lord's love and strength abounds

The Lord will overcome and take back His election

Claim Yours!!

Sandra A. Fergins

HE'S COMING BACK

Help is on the way
Be patient
Keep your faith day to day
Be patient
We often don't understand
Have faith
The Master's magnificent plan
Have faith
All of His journey for mankind is constantly unfolding
before our very eyes
Be patient
Have faith
It is going according to His plan
Wait, wait and wait some more
Wait...wait and wait some more

In The Cradle Of God's Arms

WHAT A HAPPY DAY!

The finish line into eternity
we have finally reached
Oh what a happy day that will be
We will jump, shout and praise His name
We will cry, scream and glorify His fame
for in His presence we now behold
We will tell our story of how we finally crossed over
into this glorious land eyes have not seen
Oh Lord, oh Lord you prepared such a beautiful place
for the saints so unworthy to partake

Thank you!   Thank you!! Thank you!!

Sandra A. Fergins

REACH OUT

A kind word
A kind deed
touches a lost soul indeed
An uplifting message
An unexpected show of concern
is what many helpless souls yearn
Look around, look around
someone who needs your help
can be found

In The Cradle Of God's Arms

SERVE, LIVE, TRY HIM

There is joy in the Lord
Serve Him
There is peace in the Lord
Live for Him
There is contentment in the Lord
Try Him

My brother Howard

Sandra A. Fergins

NO ONE LIKE YOU

Beautiful is His name
Wonderful, counselor
King of kings, Lord of Lords
There is no one like you
No and never will be
Man can't take your fame no matter how hard He tries
Your blueprint for life has already been laid out for each and every soul on earth
You were at the beginning of time and you are present now
You will be there in all your shining glory at the end of time

In The Cradle Of God's Arms

STAY STRONG

The world is getting dark
Mankind's love for one another slowly ebbing away
Keep your head up
Keep your faith no matter how the darkness falls
The Lord hears our faintest cries
He's there for us
His love never fails
Stay strong in His word

Sandra A. Fergins

BE GRATEFUL

I'm grateful for the victories won
For your love, patience and Christ Jesus
your son
What would I be
Where would I go
Without your direction
life would be so, so low

A JOURNEY

Another day's journey in the Lord
Life, breath and good health
We can't take anything for granted
Be thankful
Strive to be thankful

Sandra A. Fergins

POWER

Power in meeting Him
Power in knowing Him
Power in living for the Lord
Strength in a testimony
Strength in a clean life
Strength in waiting for Christ's return

In The Cradle Of God's Arms

A BLESSING

You gave me life today
A day I have never witnessed before
Each day is one to cherish
Yesterday is gone forevermore

Family food gathering!
back row: Tasha Bell, Mike Fergins Jr., Marcy Fergins
front row: Jaylen Allen, Kenneth Jackson, Reginal Ryan and
Rocco DeMore

Sandra A. Fergins

DEATH

What is coming after me
What is coming to take me away
One step behind me his name is
Death
I don't see him
I don't feel him but I know he's there
He can only be released to take me when
the Lord says my time is up
The Lord said don't fear death my child
The power of life and death is in my hand
Keep moving
Keep living
Keep reading my word
Your time will be up only when I command

In The Cradle Of God's Arms

WHY?

Why so much sadness
Why so much hate
Why so much sickness, suffering more hate
Why so much poverty
Why so much hunger
Why so much suffering more hate
My God sits high watching His creation below
He is oh so aware of man's constant despair
and will lift suffering, sickness and despair when we no longer
can bare
He knows, He knows, He knows

Sandra A. Fergins

JUST WAIT

Trials come, trials go
He's watching us all down below
Somethings we don't understand
Keep holding on to His loving, caring hand
He promised to never leave us nor forsake
A heavenly home is waiting for us to partake

In The Cradle Of God's Arms

GOD'S CREATION

Creation what a chore
Raging seas from shore to shore
Mountains, hills and valleys too
God created them for me and you
Massive whales and creeping things
Beautiful birds to trill and sing
Lastly He created man then woman for His praise
Look man, look woman
Look all around at the ungrateful hell we have raised

Sandra A. Fergins

TIME

Time is but a week, day, hour, minute or second
It ticks constantly away, away
We are here but for a moment
We look around as the years go by and wonder
where did all the time go
We can never regain the past
Live, love, give to others
while you have the time

In The Cradle Of God's Arms

GET BACK

Under attack
Devil get back
You can't keep me down
When that evil spirit surrounds
I will hold on to God's hand
The one who will help me to stand
Some days I don't comprehend
But with your grace I will win
Under attack
Devil you better GET BACK!

Sandra A. Fergins

WHAT'S HAPPENING

Fires, storms disease everywhere
Please Lord keep me in your care
Man's sinful ways are out of control
So sad
You send love's warning
has the world gone mad
Wake up people from this sleepy daze
The Lord's giving you a chance to escape this maze
Pray, cry out, get on your rusty knees
Show the Lord it is Him you want to please

In The Cradle Of God's Arms

GOD'S PEACE

The peace of God can't be surpassed
It's here for man to last and last
Some seek peace in fruitless ways
Going here and there from day to day
Turn around for the peace you seek is here for the
asking for the strong and the weak

My grandkids were my background singers on a video we did!

Sandra A. Fergins

A FRIEND'S LIFE HAS ENDED

God gave him to you
Here on earth he had but a short work to do
The love he shared can't be compared
His suffering is over now
but the imprint of his life
reigns on by the stand for
Christ he vowed

In The Cradle Of God's Arms

A BRIGHT AND WONDERFUL DAY

A new day is ahead
Don't get caught up in the gloom of life
Dark days only last for a season
Look up to the light of day
that peeks through the sky like a shining ray
Brighter days are on the way

Sandra A. Fergins

OUR HEAVENLY HOME

What a day to finally behold the Savior's face
Our journey is finally over
We completed the race
No more suffering, trials or pain
Our heavenly home we have gained
Endless smiles, laughter, happiness all around
Joy, pure joy of reaching our final destination abounds

LOOK UP

Jesus is the light of the world
Satan holds the darkness
Lift up the Lord through trials and tribulations
Don't let the weight of the world hold you down

Sandra A. Fergins

ANOTHER DAY

Another day you gave to me
One I'm forever grateful to see
Some did not make it through the night
Though they tried to hold on with all their might
Life is precious don't take it for granted
It is a gift given one day, one hour one minute
at a time

In The Cradle Of God's Arms

YOUR ANSWER

God is all we ever need
Listen to His call and heed
When we pray be patient an answer is coming
That answer often feels like an eternity but….

it is coming

My granddaughter, Dezarae with her dad, Dez Fernandez

Sandra A. Fergins

WAIT

Just to know Him
Just to see Him in peace
The time is near
Hold on a little while longer

In The Cradle Of God's Arms

THERE FOR YOU

God will lift you like no other
Look to Him
He truly cares
When you feel oh so burdened
Hold your head up
His love He'll share

Some days are filled with highs and lows
He puts them there for us to grow

Keep on praying don't stop
Relief is coming
It's on it's way

Sandra A. Fergins

A DAY

You gave me life today
A day I have never witnessed before
Each day is one to cherish
Yesterday is gone forevermore

THE BEST IS YET TO COME

Stay steady, stay calm
The best for us lies within God's palm
He knows our fears our hopes and sorrows
A better day lies in tomorrow
When you want to quit because things don't go your way
Hold on there awaits a brighter day
It's coming for you my dear friend
Be patient, be patient

Sandra A. Fergins

CHILDREN

Children are a precious sight
They often seek approval with all their might
Give them that small dose of attention they seek
That beautiful grin will often fill your spirit for more than a week
Build up that child's self-esteem with love
He will soar in growth like a morning dove

HE'S CALLING US

He speaks to all begging us to heed His call
Shaking up this sinful earth through fires, windstorms, earthquakes erupting the turf
Wake up man listen to His call
Open your eyes and ears
He wants you to not fall
The devil is near trying daily to keep you off track
The Lord says listen put down your sin-filled ways
I have your back

Sandra A. Fergins

WAKE UP

A new day is ahead
Don't get caught up in the gloom of life
Dark days only last for a season
Look up to the light of day
That peeks through the sky like a shining ray
Brighter days are on the way

In The Cradle Of God's Arms

IN HIS ARMS

God holds us in the cradle of His arms
Watching over us keeping us from harm

My nephew, Evan with his Dad Gino Orlandi and myself!

Sandra A. Fergins

YOUR ANSWER IS COMING

God is all we ever need
Listen to His call and heed
When we pray be patient an answer is coming
That answer often feels like an eternity
but….

it is coming

When life is like a raging sea
God can calm it to a whisper

In The Cradle Of God's Arms

STAY READY

Life one day
Death the next
Get ready, stay ready to ascend to your eternal home
Joy awaits
Sadness and grief swept away
Into Jesus loving arms forever to stay

Sandra A. Fergins

BLESSED

We are blessed beyond measure
Waiting to receive His treasure
Be thankful each and every day
For He has guided your way
To meet Him in peace
Once your days on earth forever cease

In The Cradle Of God's Arms

SHELTER FROM THE STORMS

Are you on the street
Do you feel defeat
I have shelter from the storms
Life brings up days sometimes down I refuse to let those uncertain times faze
I have shelter from the storms
Look up to the heavens
All things work together for a reason
This just may be your season
I have shelter from the storms
Troubles don't last always
Good times shine like beautiful sun rays
Call on the Lord with every ounce of your breath
He's all around from the highest mountains to the lowest depths
I have shelter from the storms
I called tearfully on the Lord one day to please, please hear my earnest plea

Sandra A. Fergins

He heard my cry and now a new life I see
I now know how to weather each storm
because through Christ
I have shelter from the storms

*Fun former co-workers from Ft. Sam Houston Elementary
Andrea Garcia, Michelle Schiebel and Vicki Feil!*

IT'S OKAY

It's okay to laugh at the fond memories
of old times past
It's okay to cry because you miss those good old days
that went by too fast
Go ahead laugh, cry, shout and sing
Much needed relief those
emotions will bring

Sandra A. Fergins

LOOK TO HIM

May you all be a blessed comfort to one another
May He look down over you
May He send grace to help you through
when life's problems overwhelm
My God stands strong at the helm
He is a loving kind friend
Who will hold you up until the end
Look to God don't give in
His grace is sufficient… believe

BLESSED BEYOND MEASURE

What a great day to be alive
to see the sky
Look up and pretend to fly
What a great day of good health
to enjoy living in America's abundant wealth
We have more than we can imagine
More than we deserve
Look around, look around
God has blessed us beyond measure
with so many earthly treasures
These treasures will soon past for He said
in His word they will not last

Smile and say
What a great day!

Sandra A. Fergins

THE RAIN

I hear the rain with its soft pitter, patter
as it joyfully brings great joy and laughter
It feeds the terrain washes the streets in a musical refrain
As cars dash high waves of water down the drain
Here comes loud claps of thunder
Makes the sky light up in a gentle rumble
What a beautiful sight to behold
Only God's amazing work so magnificent
for the young and old
The rain, the beautiful rain

GUIDE ME

A new year I've lived to see
One you've long ago predestined for me
Thank you for the love you've shown
Guide me this year
through the unknown

Mark 4:40
And He saith unto them, Why are ye so fearful?
How is it that ye have no faith?

Sandra A. Fergins

NO WIN

You bad make others sad
But you aren't going to win
You tear down walls
laugh when you make souls fall
But you aren't going to win
You lead souls down the wrong path
Spew out your dividing hateful wrath
But you aren't going to win
You spread miserable fires
Create biased liars
But you aren't going to win
My God is stronger, wiser than you'll ever be
because satan you had your chance to live and see
a marvelous, joyous life riches unexplainable
You gave it up for what??

YOU AREN'T GOING TO WIN!!!

In The Cradle Of God's Arms

THE RIGHT PATH

God has the best plan for our life
Oftentimes life is filled with envy, bitterness and strife
Christ can clean up those downtrodden, hurtful ways
Lead you on a clean, clear path you won't regret and want to stay
Won't you give Him a try?

My grandson AllieRay and I

Sandra A. Fergins

UNITY

In Christ there is no division
He loves us one and all
In Christ there is no color
We all are the same in His sight
In Christ there is no one pitted against another
He does not divide
only unites

In The Cradle Of God's Arms

A PROBLEM SOLVER

Are you feeling mad, sad
down in the dumps
Take your problems to the chief healer, Jesus
to get you over the hump

Sandra A. Fergins

THERE FOR US

Hateful world
Hateful times
Hateful ones around us
But GOD still reigns
Some don't share
Some don't care
We find them all around us
God still reigns above all
Take your problems to Him
He's there for us with a listening ear

In The Cradle Of God's Arms

THE RAIN

The rain cleansed the earth like quiet tears shed in fear
The soft pitter patter beating gently far, far away I hear
What a welcome sight to listen to the rain
Open the curtains wide
Let it wash away any pain
Look out onto the sidewalk people hurriedly walk by
to escape the gentle soothing raindrops as
they fall from the sky
Oh, the comforting rain

God gives you the wisdom to gain freedom!!
You are victorious from satan's grip!!

Sandra A. Fergins

IN THE CRADLE OF GOD'S ARMS

Rock me in the cradle of your arms Lord
Keep me from all hurt and harm
Your loving care I depend
Help each day I know you will send

My daughter Kendra with her husband Allen Searcey

In The Cradle Of God's Arms

HOPE

Hope for tomorrow
Hope now
Man leans on having a hope
It grows inside like a plant ever so tall
It is something we can never shake
Without hope where would we be
We would wither and die like a forlorn tree

Sandra A. Fergins

BETTER DAYS

Some days are up, happy full of life
Other days are long, confusing scattered all around
Look at those days as just the way life is sometimes
Better days are ahead
Better days are ahead

In The Cradle Of God's Arms

CHRIST CAN FIX IT

Homeless, drug ridden, cast down in despair
Christ can turn your life around and make an eternal repair

Sandra A. Fergins

NONE OTHER

No one like you Lord
No one at all
Never will be
Never has been
Man may try to rewrite, change your course
You'll set them straight with great force
You hold the keys to the kingdom
The ground work for salvation has already been won
By giving your life for all
The price has been paid

In The Cradle Of God's Arms

THE BIBLE

The bible what a wonderful book
to powerful to overlook
The words fly off the pages
Showing how life goes through many stages
This book is a comfort, a guide a lifeline
Stories, words of encouragement you will find
Let this book be a part of your daily lifeline
Read it often from week to week

My beautiful grandkids!

Sandra A. Fergins

IN HIS ARMS

May the Lord cradle you in His arms each moment
May He collect those tears you shed
He knows how dear our loved ones
He will hold you ever so near

In The Cradle Of God's Arms

CONNECT

Division, lies the devil creates
The Lord can break that tension
Connect with Him through prayer

My daughter, Marcy Fergins, and my sister, Angela Medearis

Sandra A. Fergins

GOD'S THERE

Evil all around
God's love forever abounds
He's there for us
He cares for us
When things don't go your way
He can lift you up make a better day

In The Cradle Of God's Arms

GONE AWAY

A special friend God gave to you
He's gone away, away too soon
You've cried and laughed
Cherished special times
But now those days too soon have passed

Sandra A. Fergins

WAITING FOR YOU

The world is getting bleak
Is it help you seek
Is it an answer unknown
to a world so cold has grown
Look above help is near
As you quietly shed a tear
He awaits with open arms
Wanting to keep you from all harm

In The Cradle Of God's Arms

HE'S HERE FOR US

My God is my protector
My friend in time of need
When I need an uplift
He sends my way relief
Jesus is the answer for the world today
No matter how man ignores Him
His word is here to stay

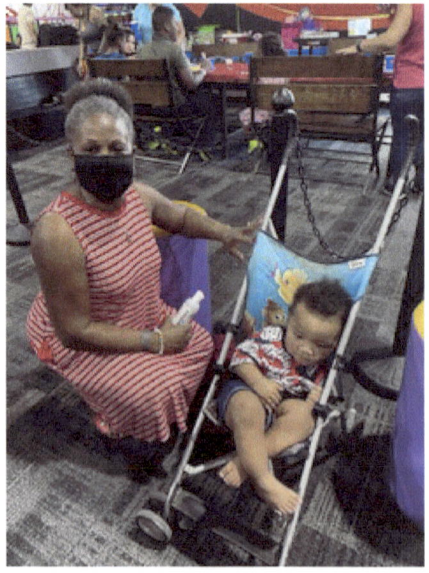

Yvonne and AllieRay

Sandra A. Fergins

IT'S COMING

Death is but one step away
It's on it's way
Come what may
Daily we must constantly prepare
The love of God willingly share
He did not say everyday would be easy or light
But through His love He'll give you strength to satan fight
Soon it will all be over and we'll take….. our final flight

GONE ON

A loved one has gone on
inside we feel so torn
Sometimes we feel so out of place
In time remember the almighty God and saints you'll meet face to face
What a glorious time it will be
To walk on those streets of gold and to behold indescribable, breathtaking wonders
That day is not far off

Sandra A. Fergins

FEELINGS

Everyone has feelings
whether big or small
Everyone wants love
share yours over all
Reach out, extend yourself
Near and far all about
You'll touch someone with love so dear
Helping to erase their inner, pent up fears

1 John 4:11
*Beloved, if God so loved us, we ought also to
love one another.*

In The Cradle Of God's Arms

MOTHER

What is a mother
A soul that gives and gives and gives
What is a mother
One who wants to see her children and loved ones thrive and live
You are that special mother
A mother to the young and old
One whose love is everlasting
A love that grows daily and will never grow cold

Love you

My mom, Angeline

Sandra A. Fergins

DAUGHTERS

What are daughters
beautiful souls
Ones that are wonderful to behold
What are daughters
Ones that I've loved and cherished from birth
Ones that I've laughed, cried and played with from the beginning 'till now
I love having you both as my special daughters and
I always will
Keep growing and loving the Lord until the very end
Love Mom

    Dedicated to my daughters Kendra Searcy & Marcy Fergins

In The Cradle Of God's Arms

SNOW

Beautiful white powder
falls swiftly to the ground
Swirling and twirling landing softly making mounds
Snow beautiful snow piling high
Bringing smiles and sighs from the young and old
Carefully we trek outside to touch this amazing creation
Making snowmen and snowballs
What an ultimate sensation

This event occurred 2/14/21 through 2/18/21 in the lone star state of Texas. WOW!!

Sandra A. Fergins

PLOP!

The beautiful white snow has turned a mushy brown
Cars and feet have pounced on it all over town
Slowly it melts over time
Turning into a soft wet slime
Chunks of ice fall from cars and rooftops
Plop, plop, plop

*My first book signing of my first book
"There's No Better Friend... Jesus!!
I was so excited!!*

AWAKE

The morning awakes so gently
No longer is it night
The birds and squirrels awake from their rest
Scrounge for food at best
The houses light up slowly
Car motors rev up for a drive
Once again the cycle of life begins
When the morning awakes once again
So happy to be...alive

John 14:27
Peace I leave with you, my peace I give unto you: not as the world giveth, give I unto you. Let not your heart be troubled, neither let it be afraid.

Sandra A. Fergins

A BETTER DAY

Bear your burdens big or small
God will cover them all and all
Sometimes the weight feels like more
than we can bear
God is over one and all
and He truly cares
When life has you under a strain
In time God will lift that heavy rain
Wait, wait and wait some more
A better day He has in store

In The Cradle Of God's Arms

TROUBLES DON'T LAST

Whenever you are feeling down
Look up one day you are going to
wear a golden crown
Whenever you are feeling weary and teary
Your day is coming soon to feel light and cheery
Hold fast, troubles don't always last

II Corinthians 1:4
Who comforteth us in all our tribulation, that we may be able to comfort them which are in any trouble, by the comfort wherewith we ourselves are comforted of God.

Sandra A. Fergins

GRATEFUL

God woke me up this morning feeling fine
Basking in the radiant sunshine
What will I do with the day He has given
Tell Him I'm oh so grateful to be
amongst the living

In The Cradle Of God's Arms

THERE FOR YOU

Evil all around
God's love forever abounds
He's there for us
He cares for us
When things don't go your way
He can lift you up and make a better day

Sandra A. Fergins

GONE AWAY

A special friend God gave to you
Their gone away, away too soon
You've cried and laughed
cherished special times
But now those days
too soon have passed

Hanging out with my fast car

In The Cradle Of God's Arms

MY CHILDREN

Children so precious
so gentle so sweet
From their wavy hair to their little feet
They grow into toddlers wobbling around
Stumble ever so slightly down to the ground
Off to school to meet new friends we ride
As tears I hide on the inside
A whirlwind of school activities through the years
The time I have with them I hold so dear
Children are precious
No matter what profession they take
We give and give hoping the best for goodness sake

Matthew 19:14
But Jesus said, Suffer little children, and forbid them not, to come unto me: for of such is the kingdom of heaven.

Sandra A. Fergins

FAITH

Faith can conquer all your fears
Just put all your trust in Him
When you're feeling down
Almost leveled to the ground
Look up my God is near

In The Cradle Of God's Arms

SEEKING ANSWERS

The world is getting bleak
Is it help you seek
Is it an answer unknown
to a world so cold has grown
Look above help is near
As you quietly shed a tear
He awaits with open arms
Wanting to keep you from all harm

Sandra A. Fergins

LONELY TRIALS

The Lord will hold you up through your lonely days,
Through your lonely nights He's there for you
This is just a trial called life
Lean on Him every step of the way
No matter what others do or say

Matthew 28:20
Teaching them to observe all things whatsoever
I have commanded you: and, lo, I am with you
always, even unto the end of the world. Amen

Matthew 22:14
For many are called, but few are chosen.

In The Cradle Of God's Arms

LOOK FORWARD

What a wonder to behold
More precious than pure gold
When our loving Savior we meet
To fall at His precious feet
To retell the stories of old
Of how He gave us grace to stand tall and bold
No one is like the one above
Who showers us with so much love
What a day, what a day
What a happy day it will be
When His glorious face we will see

John 6:28
Jesus answered and said unto them, This is the work of God, that ye believe on him whom he hath sent.

Sandra A. Fergins

SURRENDER

The lightening roars
God's voice soars
Our attention peaks
Glory He seeks
Man's love He hates to lose
He constantly warns us the right path to choose
Look to God for the love you seek
He's waiting for the lost
to surrender to Him with open arms
week to week

In The Cradle Of God's Arms

YOU MATTER TO GOD

No matter what the world around
you displays

Rocco with her dad William DeMore.

Sandra A. Fergins

LIFE?? DEATH??

Life
Laughter, smiles, fears
Death
sadness, grief, tears
Life is an emotional roller coaster at times
witnessing good days and bad days
Cities filled with crime
How do we cope
People without hope
Turning to dope
Look to Jesus
He's not far away
Ask Him to come into your heart and forever stay today

PAIN

Pain a part of the aging process
We can't get around it no matter our success
It is good to know in prayer we can always go
to the Lord above
to one day send relief
to His children suffering in grief

Sandra A. Fergins

GRIEF

Another day of silent grief
Lord oh Lord when will you send relief
To you I know I can always go
But this trial of patience seems to have no end
I'm patiently waiting for your relief to send
Some days I shout out
cry, seeking pity
So loud my voice seems to reach within the city
I know this is a much needed test
One day soon I will receive
sweet…..rest

In The Cradle Of God's Arms

CHILDHOOD

Enjoy your childhood every day
No matter what others do or say
Play, run, enjoy the sun
Your life of fun has just begun
One day you'll look back on days gone past
You'll smile and say
They went….. mighty fast

Sandra A. Fergins

ALLIERAY
(My Youngest Grandson AllieRay Searcy)

AllieRay has something to say

every single day

He coos and woos

Kicks off his shoes

Flashes a toothless smile

A smile so wide

beamed with pride

Makes one laugh until you cry

A child so precious and so dear

God knows His strengths and every fear

My grandson AllieRay.

In The Cradle Of God's Arms

THE BIBLE

The bible is God's love letter to us
In His word we must trust
In His word daily seek
Strength you'll gain
week to week

I had a lot of great times with my former co-worker Evelyn Narcisse.

Sandra A. Fergins

THERE FOR YOU

He's there for you
He's there for you
When you don't quite understand
What life has thrown your way
God will pick you up
in due time
Turn your frown into a smile
Patiently wait
Patiently wait
For my God is there for you

IN HIS TIME

It was His love for me
that spared my life
He looked down from above and said
come my child
He had a master plan for me to follow through
A set date and time to
walk this Christian life

Sandra A. Fergins

WATER

The water beneath our feet
is calm
brings needed relief
Swaying back and forth
rising in a beautiful
crescendo of sounds
Under the water
the sand crunches with every step taken
leaving temporary footprints behind
The water swirls and curls back and forth in a
beautiful dance of its own
We bask in this cool, cool water for any
feeling of melancholy is whisked away
leaving all in a beautiful state of euphoria

Leave your worries to the Lord
Leave them there and let them be

NATURE

The birds sing gaily
Their daily life has begun once more
Singing, gliding, playfully through the trees
enjoying every moment
They understand their chorus like melodies to one another
What a wonder to behold
Enjoy, take in nature's mysteries
This new day once more

Sandra A. Fergins

THE HOSPITAL

In the hospital
No rest, no rest
They come and go
Ask questions so
What's a patient to do
Don't stay sick
Get better quick
Or you might be there another week

In The Cradle Of God's Arms

HIS LOVE

It was His love for me that spared my life
He looked down from above and said,
    "Come my child."
He had a master plan for me to follow through
A set date and time to walk a Christian life

My brother-in-law Michael Medearis

Sandra A. Fergins

IF

If it had not been for Christ saving me
If it had not been for His endless love
If it had not been for His sacrifice for me
Where would I be in this lonely world
What would I do
Thank you Lord for choosing me

LOOKING FOR PEACE

You too can find peace
within your soul
You too can find peace
don't let your heart grow cold

Sandra A. Fergins

THAT HOPELESS FEELING

When you feel in despair
Help is on the way
God loves mankind and truly cares
When life is making you feel confused
and lost
Turn your life over to Jesus count up the cost
He will make your pathways straight
He wants you to enter those pearly gates

In The Cradle Of God's Arms

THERE FOR YOU

In sickness
He's there
In good health
He's there
Patiently wait for that answered
prayer

Jeremiah 17:14
Heal me, O Lord, and I shall be healed; save me,
and I shall be saved: for thou art my praise.

Sandra A. Fergins

TELL IT

Tell His story
don't be ashamed
He's known near and far
A marquee of fame
Tell His story
Healing the sick raising the dead
No qualms or fears
He did it without dread
Tell His story
Shout it across the billowy skies
Let the world know after three days in the grave
He did rise
Tell His story
Stand proud stand bold
Jesus' story is the greatest story ever told

In The Cradle Of God's Arms

AN ENDING

Each of us has an ending moment
Each of us has a last day
Live each day with love and grace
God will help you run this race
Don't worry
Don't fret
Your lifelong steps have been set
His magnificent plan for each of His creation has been laid out long ago
In due time the things we see asunder
We will no longer have to wonder

My son, Mike Jr., Rocco, Kenneth and my husband Michael.

Sandra A. Fergins

WHAT ARE YOU WAITING FOR

He's right there
I know He cares
Patiently waiting
His love to share
What are you waiting for
With a new Christian life you too can soar
Higher heights you will gain
Leave that old sinful life behind that brought
so much pain
A new clean life you will regain

MARRIAGE

Marriage was created by God
He joins two hearts to forever be bound
There are good days
There are bad
There are days you laugh and cry together
There are days you have to hold one another up
You are a forever team
You must weather each storm through sickness and health
For richer for poorer
He and only He will give you the help you need to hold each other up
Till that last dying breath

Ephesians 5:28
So ought men to love their wives as their own bodies. He that loveth his wife loveth himself.

Sandra A. Fergins

TREES

Trees, trees
What a beautiful sight
A portrait of colors by day and by night
Some rock and sway in a dance
of the breeze
Others shed leaves in winter falling gently
with ease
Soon spring quietly tiptoes in
And the cycle of tree life begins again

NATURE

On a clear day the gentle breeze blows
moving the billowy clouds
setting the hillsides all aglow
the stream moves slowly through the terrain
in a gentle flow
as the butterflies flit from plant to plant
in a colorful wing dance ever so slow
we breathe in the wind
that we cannot see
and watch as the birds fly from tree to tree
what a beautiful sight to behold
this nature God created is like pure gold

Sandra A. Fergins

RAIN

I love the sound of the rain
Clouds collide
The gentle roar
The raindrops make a tinkling sound
as they make their way down, down
to the ground
Scenes of childhood dance in my head
of days gone past
boots splashing in the rain
What a wonderful feeling of joy the rain brings
as we listen to the pitter, patter sound
of another rainy day

In The Cradle Of God's Arms

LIGHTNING

The lightning flash illuminates the sky
as the clouds laugh and rumble
shaking walls as they roar by
What a sight
What a sound
Oh what a beauty to behold
as we watch the sky light up and darken
and the gentle raindrops fall

Sandra A. Fergins

OLD AGE

Getting old
turning grey
We can't avoid it
come what may
Next the stubborn weight suddenly appears
The weight wants to stay
On no, oh dear
you try this diet and exercise every which way
Those extra pounds just won't go away
Suddenly things seem blurry, reading glasses await
You wonder, what next is my fate
The teeth you lose one by one
The dentist says try these expensive implants, hon
One day in the mirror you see sagging jaws and a wrinkly neck
The aging process is here to stay

Oh Heck!

In The Cradle Of God's Arms

He's there for you
God cares for you
The most loving friend you
could ever have!

1 John 4:19
We love Him, because He first loved us.

My sister, Marcia and nephew Evan.

Sandra A. Fergins

THE REUNION

The reunion what a day
You look forward to it or wish it would go away
Will they recognize me
Or ask my name as if they can't see
The weight gain was inevitable
The aging process set in…… see
If I could turn back the hands of time
I would, that's not a crime
The bags and wrinkles
The flabby skin
More and more wrinkles
when I flash my famous grin
Some I know are on a cane
When I knew them years ago we were jealous of their fame
Others have put on quite a waist
We can tell they have an unquenchable taste
Alas, where did the hair go
some wore it long, thick or in an afro
Now its grey, bald or mighty thin

In The Cradle Of God's Arms

As time goes on enjoy your new look
With your life wisdom you can fill a book

Psalm 71:9
Cast me not off in the time of old age; forsake me not when my strength faileth.

Proverbs 10:27
The fear of the Lord prolongeth days: but the years of the wicked shall be shortened.

I Corinthians 2:9
But as it is written. Eye hath not seen, nor ear heard, neither have entered into the heart of man, the things which God hath prepared for them that love him.

Sandra A. Fergins

THERE FOR YOU

Reach out to Him
extend your hand
God has a magnificent plan
One well written by Him alone
Because you my child to Him belong
He is the great I am
a master of all
Lean and depend on Him
He won't let you fall

In The Cradle Of God's Arms

HELP

Help me to find my purpose Lord
Help me to do it well
I want to please you Lord
I don't want to go to HELL!!

My husband and I.

Sandra A. Fergins

SHOES

If my shoes could talk
They would say take me for a relaxing walk
Don't leave me in the closet so long
That tennis shoe over there smells mighty strong
Don't you realize I vie to be on your feet
Try me on some time
Dance with me
I can keep a steady beat
I hate being left alone
I've been in this same spot far too long
Take me out for a spin
With the comfort of these soles you are bound to WIN!!

In The Cradle Of God's Arms

A MIRACLE

What is a miracle
God's power manifested through Him and Him alone
Something for the world to see
Something brightly shone
You can't explain a miracle
No matter how you try
It brings you to tears
His love makes you cry
A miracle can't be explained
It is God's working power
It is His way of sending His love in a peaceful, gentle shower

(Inspired by a plane that burst into flames heading for takeoff near Houston, Texas carrying 21 passengers and all survived.) October 2021

Sandra A. Fergins

STOP THE VIOLENCE

We've got to stop the violence
Bullets kill everyday
Please listen closely to what I say
Packing guns is not cool
I'm sure you've heard this
In or out of school
Guns can lead you to an early grave
Please listen to these words
You it may save
Ugly words can lead to an unnecessary fight
You think pulling out a gun is out of sight
You've got it wrong
Read the bible, staying in God's word, keeps your mind strong
The devil laughs when you pick up that gun
He says, "I've got one more fool, cool."

In The Cradle Of God's Arms

A TEACHER

I am a teacher
I work with tall and small
Some days I ache for goodness sake
But I trudge on without a grudge
I am a teacher
I've been told all minds I mold
Whether for a short span or long
I know I can
Some days this job is loads of fun
Other days you want to go off and run
I am a teacher
Appreciated by all some days
Other times you feel like a gerbil in a maze
I am a teacher
Created by the Lord above
Sent to earth to give of my love

Sandra A. Fergins

Proverbs 3:6
In all thy ways acknowledge Him, and
He shall direct thy paths.

Psalm 49:14
For this God is our God for ever and ever:
He will be our guide even unto death.

In The Cradle Of God's Arms

WRONG PERSON

I didn't do it ma
Her child lets off a loud wail
He resists to being pulled slowly off to jail
Please ma, hear me
I didn't do it
The anklets jingle loudly as he's led to a grisly cell
Hear me out, believe me
Please ma, believe me
One more crime pinned on the wrong child
in a hasty, shabby conviction of being of the darker race
Mama, his voice faintly drifts away
Hopefully, his case will be retried soon,
real soon another day

Sandra A. Fergins

THE COVID BLUES

I've got the covid blues
Sick and tired of the news
I've got the covid blues
Day and night in my houseshoes
I've got the covid blues
Stores say stay within six feet
Limited places to eat
Small gatherings for a few
People what are we to do
Masks shortage, masks abundance
No more smiles you'll see for a while
People sick every week
Dying here dying there
People dying everywhere
Schools closed, streets froze
Unusual weather, too cold for gatherings
What are we to do
Throw our hands up in distress
Walk around head hung down depressed
No, this is our time to heed God's wake up call

In The Cradle Of God's Arms

He desires none of His children to fall
A better day lies ahead
through His gospel our souls are fed
Read, pray commune daily with the Lord
Your hungry soul will be fed

My son Kenneth, grandson K. J. and me on Thanksgiving.

Sandra A. Fergins

GET RIGHT

Babies crying
Soldiers dying
Tragic losses everywhere
People seem like they don't care
Love among the races slowly ebbing away
Disasters everywhere you look
This old earth being constantly shook
Sin has a devastating affect on people's minds
The majority favors not being ever so kind
God is well aware not wanting to lose not one soul
Stand up, Get Right come out of the cold
A better life by serving God is the only way out of this mess
Look up my friend take the narrow road to life's victory
Show the world you chose to serve God
He is the best!!

In The Cradle Of God's Arms

SKIT

THE UNEXPECTED EVENT

Setting : Two friends in a coffee shop.
They have known each other for quite awhile.

Characters : Pearl and Candace

Scene 1

Pearl : It is so good that you could break out of the house today.

Candace : I know, I enjoy the coffee here and the great service.

Pearl : I need prayer.

Candace : (Jokingly) Oh, What's wrong dear.

Pearl : I haven't been feeling my usual self.

Candace : (Still talking playfully) Usual self, usual self? Do you mean everything is working right? No joint pains, headaches, toe aches, gas?

Pearl : All right girl, don't you go there. I haven't been feeling like I'm a teen again but I probably just need a little more rest.

Candace : (Still said in joking fashion) Yeah, rest, exercise, diet. More rest, exercise, diet.
Pearl : Okay, I've got it. Don't go there. I do have some good news.
Candace : Tell me quick before I have to repeat myself.
Pearl : My son, Jamir is coming home on leave in a few days.
Candace : Wow! I know you are excited. How long has it been since you last saw Jamir.
Pearl : It's been almost two years. We talk on the phone and he e-mails me.
Candace : Fancy, fancy, the e-mail lady.
Pearl : Be quiet. I have kept up with the computer age. I even take classes to keep up with new advances every now and then.
Candace : You don't say. Ms. Techy, Steve Jobs
Pearl : Don't you go there. I mentioned to you awhile back I was taking a few classes. I even mention to you when he calls. Anyway, I'm getting his room all ready for him. He says he'll be on leave two weeks.
Candace : I bet you already have your breakfast, lunch and dinner menus planned out. You've probably been to the store ten times all ready.
Pearl : No, I haven't but I did make a menu.
Candace : Oh wow. Am I invited over for one of those days?

In The Cradle Of God's Arms

Pearl : Of course. Come over anytime you want. You know you don't need an invitation.

Candace : Okay. Well I am going to let you get back to your preparations for this special occasion. I'll be waiting to hear from you. Enjoy the rest of your day.

Pearl : You too. See you soon.

They leave coffee shop.

As soon as Candace returns home she receives a call from Pearl.

Scene 2

Pearl : (Talking hysterically) I just got a call from a Col. Baker. Jamir's commanding officer. He says Jamir has been injured badly from a sneak attack on his squadron. He's in the hospital now. I am so upset. (crying) He didn't give many details.

Candace : Okay, Okay. Getting worried is what the devil wants you to do. Once you do that you're not showing the Lord you have faith.

Pearl : (crying) I do have faith. I do have faith. I really do.

Candace : At this moment we can't do anything but pray and hope for the best. The Lord is working according to His will not ours. It was predestinated for this to happen.

Pearl : I know (sobbing) but he's my baby. I don't want anything to happen to Jamir.

Candace : And, it won't. Trust, believe receive.

Two weeks later they meet up at the coffee shop.

Pearl : Good to see you Candace.

Candace : It is nice to meet up with you.

Pearl's phone rings. She quickly grabs it. She breaks into a wide smile while listening to caller.

Pearl : It was Jamir's commanding officer. He says Jamir is clear to fly home and should be here in two days.

They both shriek with laughter.

Candace : Great news! Great news! God is so good. I am so happy for you and Jamir!

Pearl : Praise God! I AM TOO!

THE END

In The Cradle Of God's Arms

SKIT 2

THE CHANGE

A group of old friends preparing for the new school year. One has made a life altering change.

Five characters

Character 1 : Summer was great! I really look forward to starting school this year. Being in that new environment will be really something! I can't wait.

Character 2 : Yeah! There are about 900 students in the school and sometimes its hard finding your class.

Character 3 : You get use to the change after about a week. My favorite class was biology with Ms. Harris. She wears bifocals, so sit toward the back and she won't even notice if you're eating breakfast or snacks. Just keep sliding it in your mouth like this and then pretend like you're wiping your face. She only looks towards the back about every fifteen minutes.

Character 4 : No, its every twelve minutes. I timed her one day.

Character 1 : Be sure and compliment her on what's she's wearing. She will blush from here to eternity.

(Some laugh)

Character 2 : You aren't saying much (looks at character 5) Cat got your tongue?

Character 3 : No, the way (Say **she's or he's** for the one playing the part) sitting there you would think (**she or he**) had been eaten alive! Now we're looking at (her or his) wax figure that was prepared for a museum. (They all laugh)

Character 5 : I'm all right. I'm just enjoying your conversation.

Character 4 : Are you sure?

Character 5 : Sure I'm sure

Character 3 : Are you really sure! We didn't forget our deodorant did we? (Playfully checking under their arms,)

Character 5 : No, really. My summer was great and I have good news.

Character 1 : What you've finally given your Big Bird Doll away? (all laugh)

Character 2 : No, you don't need a nightlight? (all laugh)

In The Cradle Of God's Arms

Character 5 : No. Seriously. I gave my life to Christ. I have a new walk. A new way of thinking and great joy in my heart.

Character 4 : You mean you're not going out with us on our graffiti runs on the bridge and the side of the convenience store?

Character 5 : No!

Character 2 : You're not going to shoplift with us anymore?

Character 5 : No!

Character 3 : You're not going to sneak out of the house after midnight to smoke weed?

Character 5 : NO!

All look at each other and chime in together.

All : You're no fun!!

Character 5 : I use to think those things were fun but now my life has more meaning and those deeds we did together only gave me a temporary fulfillment.

Character 1 : (grabs Character 5 by shoulders and says) Where is the old you? Where is the old you?

Character 5 : I still care about you all but I came to a crossroad in my life and I now want to live a better life. I want to grow and get to know the Lord. I want to study to show myself approved unto God.

Character 3 : You are too weird.

Character 4 : Let's get out of here

Character 1 : Check you later.

Character 2 : I'll catch up with you all later.

(Turns toward Character 5)

You really got my attention. I think I might want to visit your church some time.

Character 5 : I would love for you to hear God's word for yourself. He can do the same thing for you that He did for me. You also ought to hear the choir. We have some great singers! You know you have a great voice too!

Character 2 : I look forward to attending with you.

THE END

www.ingramcontent.com/pod-product-compliance
Lightning Source LLC
Chambersburg PA
CBHW042236090526
44589CB00006B/72